A MILLION MOVES:

KEEPING FIT

Slim Goodbody's
LIGHTEN UP
SERIES

Crabtree Publishing Company
www.crabtreebooks.com

Series Development and Packaging: John Burstein, Slim Goodbody Corp.
Senior Script Development: Phoebe Backler
Managing Editor: Valerie J. Weber
Designer and Illustrator: Ben McGinnis
Graphic Design Agency: Adventure Advertising
Instructional Designer: Alan Backler, Ph. D.
Content Consultant: Betty Hubbard, Ed. D., Certified Health Education Specialist
Project Editor: Reagan Miller

Library and Archives Canada Cataloguing in Publication

Burstein, John.
 A million moves : keeping fit / Slim Goodbody.

(Slim Goodbody's lighten up!)
ISBN 978-0-7787-3912-8 (bound).--ISBN 978-0-7787-3930-2 (pbk.)

 1. Exercise--Health aspects--Juvenile literature. 2. Physical
fitness--Juvenile literature. I. Title. II. Series: Goodbody, Slim. Slim
Goodbody's lighten up!

RA781.G66 2008   j613.7'1   C2008-900726-3

Library of Congress Cataloging-in-Publication Data

Burstein, John.
 A million moves : keeping fit / John Burstein.
    p. cm. -- (Slim goodbody's lighten up!)
 Includes index.
 ISBN-13: 978-0-7787-3912-8 (rlb)
 ISBN-10: 0-7787-3912-0 (rlb)
 ISBN-13: 978-0-7787-3930-2 (pb)
 ISBN-10: 0-7787-3930-9 (pb)
 1. Exercise--Health aspects--Juvenile literature.
 2. Physical fitness--Juvenile literature. I. Title. II. Series.

 RA781.B883 2008
 613.7'1--dc22
                                      2008003591

Crabtree Publishing Company

www.crabtreebooks.com   1-800-387-7650

Published in Canada
Crabtree Publishing
616 Welland Ave.
St. Catharines, Ontario
L2M 5V6

Published in the United States
Crabtree Publishing
PMB16A
350 Fifth Ave., Suite 3308
New York, NY 10118

Published in the United Kingdom
Crabtree Publishing
White Cross Mills
High Town, Lancaster
LA1 4XS

Published in Australia
Crabtree Publishing
386 Mt. Alexander Rd.
Ascot Vale (Melbourne)
VIC 3032

Printed in the U.S.A.

TABLE OF CONTENTS

Slim Goodbody's **LIGHTEN UP** SERIES

HELLO THERE. I'M SLIM GOODBODY,

and my greatest goal in life is to help young people across the planet become healthy and active. After all, one in three kids in the United States is overweight. Without changing their eating and exercise habits, many of these young people will become overweight adults. They risk many possible health problems like **high blood pressure** or **diabetes**.

Today, I am here to introduce you to my friend Lucas. He's working on becoming more physically fit. He wants to reach his goal and perform well in the President's Challenge at school. Join Lucas as he learns about the importance of exercise and how to reach his goals.

LUCAS VERSUS THE PRESIDENT'S CHALLENGE

Hi. My name is Lucas. I've always been the smallest kid in my class. This year, I'm determined to get stronger and run faster. In a few months, my class is going to take the President's Challenge to earn physical fitness awards in gym class. You may have had this challenge at your school. During the challenge, we'll perform exercises that test our **endurance**, strength, and **flexibility**.

I still have bad memories of trying to do pull-ups in the Challenge last year. My arms were shaking, and my friends all laughed at me. Ever since then, they've called me "Lucas the Light." It was time to ask my gym teacher, Ms. Lindsay, for advice on how to get in shape.

TO BECOME A LEAN, MEAN FITNESS MACHINE

"Hey, Ms. Lindsay," I said as I strolled into the gym.

"Hey there, Lucas. What can I do for you?" asked Ms. Lindsay.

"The President's Challenge is in ten weeks. This year, I want to be a lean, mean, fitness machine. No more 'Lucas the Light!'" I laughed.

"Alright, Lucas!" said Ms. Lindsay enthusiastically. "To prepare for the Challenge, you'll need to be physically active every day. It doesn't matter too much what you do. Playing football, running, and hip-hop dancing all strengthen your heart, muscles, and bones."

"I walk my dog every day. Does that count?" I asked.

Slim Goodbody Says: The U.S. government recommends that children and adolescents get at least 60 minutes of moderate-intensity activity most days of the week. That means that all kids should run, play soccer, go biking, or do some other kind of physically challenging exercise for one hour a day, four or more days a week.

"Well, it depends how quickly you walk. A twenty-minute stroll won't cut it," Ms. Lindsay laughed. "Take a look at this chart, Lucas. The activity pyramid is a helpful guide for anyone who wants to be healthy, strong, and physically fit."

MOVE IT FROM LESS TO ENOUGH

"You can see that watching TV, using the computer, and sitting around all fit into the *Less* category. So turn off the television and get up off the couch!

"Jogging, swimming, and jumping rope increase your heart and breathing rate. Do *More* of these kinds of exercise to get fit.

"Weight training and **resistance exercises** like carrying a heavy backpack or groceries will strengthen your bones and muscles. Those exercises fit into the *Enough* category.

"Most importantly, you need to get *Plenty* of moderate physical activity, which includes riding a bike, playing tennis, or climbing stairs. It helps a lot if you find ways to include exercise in your daily routine," Ms. Lindsay said. "Good luck, Lucas!"

WHAT'S SO GREAT ABOUT EXERCISE?

The next day, I went on the Internet to learn more about exercise and health. I remembered my teacher's advice about using web sites with addresses ending in *.edu* and *.gov*. She explained that schools and the government make those web sites. Because these groups are not trying to sell you something, the information on them is **valid** and reliable.

The first web site that I found explained that if you eat a **nutritious** diet and are physically active, you will be healthier. When you exercise, your body needs to burn more food. If you eat larger amounts of healthy food, it is easier to make sure that you are getting all of the nutrients that you need to stay healthy.

The web site also explained that if you don't get enough exercise, it is more difficult to stay at a healthy weight. If you're under- or overweight, you risk many different kinds of health problems. If you're underweight, you may not be getting the **nutrients** that your body needs to fight off illnesses. If you are overweight, you are at risk of diabetes, high blood pressure, and heart problems.

.EDU
.GOV

NUTRIENTS

Slim Goodbody Says: The key to maintaining a healthy weight is to find a balance between the **calories** that you take in from eating food and the calories that you burn through physical activity. Your body burns calories through a **metabolic process** that breaks down food and changes it into energy that your body can use. If you don't find a way to burn the calories that you eat, they are stored in your body as fat.

BLOOD: BRINGING ENERGY AND REMOVING WASTE

I kept surfing the Internet and found another site about the heart. I didn't realize that my heart pumps blood to every **cell** in my body. The blood carries nutrients and oxygen all over my body. The moving blood also gets rid of unwanted substances like **creatinine**, that is a waste product created by eating protein. The stronger your heart is, the more blood it can pump, and the healthier your body will be!

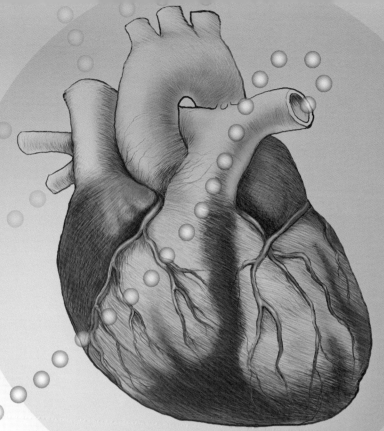

HEART

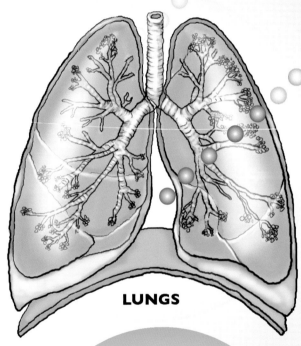

LUNGS

BREATHING BETTER

Exercise strengthens your respiratory system, too. Your **respiratory system** sends out oxygen to your body. It also releases waste gases, like carbon dioxide, that your body doesn't need. When you exercise regularly, your lungs can take in extra air each time you breathe. As a result, your body receives more oxygen, releases more carbon dioxide, and works better.

Some scientists even believe that physical activity helps keep your mind sharp and helps you learn more. Many people also use exercise to unwind and relax.

"Wow," I thought, "I guess getting in shape really is a good idea."

MIGHTY MUSCLES

The next day, I decided to go to the fitness center at the local teen club. I wanted to learn more about strengthening my muscles. I'd seen posters for their fitness center, and it seemed like a good place to start. When I arrived, I asked for help at the front desk.

"Hey there! What can I do for you, young man?" asked Fiona, the fitness-center director.

"I want to learn how to build my muscles. We have the President's Challenge coming up, and I want to be ready for it," I explained.

FIVE PARTS TO FITNESS

"Well, you came to the right place. I can help you come up with a fitness plan that will cover the five main areas of physical fitness — muscle strength, muscle endurance, heart and lung endurance, and flexibility. Where would you like to start?" asked Fiona.

"My biggest goal is to get stronger, so let's start with muscle strength," I said.

"OK. Muscle strength is the amount of force that your muscles can produce. The more you use your muscles, the stronger they will become. When your muscles are stronger, it's easier to do any kind of physical activity. Your bones also get stronger and thicker at the same time," said Fiona.

"Great! How do I get started?" I asked.

PUSH THOSE MUSCLES!

"Well, you need to find activities that allow your muscles to work against resistance. That just means that you need to lift, push, or pull something to make your muscles stronger," she said. Fiona sat down at a weight-lifting machine. Her muscles rippled as she lifted the weights above her head.

"You can come to the gym to lift weights, but there are lots of other ways to strengthen your muscles. Get creative! Walking up stairs strengthens your leg muscles. Pull-ups and push-ups build your arm muscles. If you do these exercises several times a week, you can maintain and build your muscle strength," Fiona explained. "Why don't you come back tomorrow, and we'll talk about the rest of your fitness plan?"

"Thanks, Fiona. I'll see you tomorrow," I said and started for home.

Slim Goodbody Says: Lucas can also work on curl-ups–an event in the Presidential Challenge that tests your **abdominal** strength. Why don't you try them too? Lie on cushioned, clean surface with your knees bent and feet about 12 inches (30 cm) from your body. Cross your arms over your chest, placing your hands on opposite shoulders. Have a partner hold your feet down as you lift your upper body off the floor. Lower your upper body until it just touches the floor, and start again. See how many you can do in a minute.

BUILD YOUR MUSCLE ENDURANCE

The next day, I was on my way to the fitness center. I saw my parents' friend Roger getting ready to go for a run.

"Hi, Roger," I said.

"Hey, Lucas. How are you?" Roger asked.

"Fine, thanks. You know, I always see you out exercising. Do you think that you could help me? I'm trying to get in shape in time for the President's Challenge. Last night, I did as many pushups as I could. I also did a bunch of bicep curls by lifting soup cans. I tried heel raises on the steps to strengthen my calves, too."

"Soup cans! That's a new one." Roger laughed.

"I know it sounds weird, Roger," I replied. "But it's cheaper and easier than buying a weight machine or joining a fitness center. Fiona, my fitness coach, also said that you can climb up the stairs at home for a set amount of time instead of using a stair machine. She even suggested using a pack of frozen peas to ice my sore muscles!"

"Those are great ideas, Lucas, but building your muscles is only one part of getting in shape. You also need to work on muscle endurance," Roger advised.

BICEP MUSCLE

CALF MUSCLE

AEROBIC EXERCISE BUILDS MUSCLES

"What's that?" I asked.

"If you have muscle endurance, you can use the same muscles for a long time without getting tired. I can go for long runs because my leg muscles have muscle endurance. You need to get **aerobic** exercise to build your muscle endurance," explained Roger.

"Aerobic exercise makes your body use a lot of oxygen over a long time, right?" I asked.

"Exactly. And to get aerobic exercise, you can do anything from carrying your backpack while you walk at a quick pace to riding your

bike to going for a jog. The most important thing is to find a kind of exercise that's fun. I love to go for a long run, because it clears my mind. Some people like playing team sports, swimming, or in-line skating around a park. If you find a kind of exercise that's fun for you, chances are that you'll want to keep at it," said Roger.

"Thanks, Roger. Have a good run!" I said.

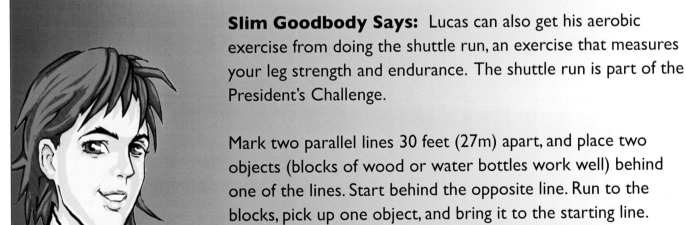

Slim Goodbody Says: Lucas can also get his aerobic exercise from doing the shuttle run, an exercise that measures your leg strength and endurance. The shuttle run is part of the President's Challenge.

Mark two parallel lines 30 feet (27m) apart, and place two objects (blocks of wood or water bottles work well) behind one of the lines. Start behind the opposite line. Run to the blocks, pick up one object, and bring it to the starting line. Repeat with the second object. Time yourself over the next few weeks. Can you do more runs in the same amount of time? Can you increase the number of runs you do before you run out of breath?

BUILD YOUR HEART AND LUNG ENDURANCE

Back at the fitness center, I found Fiona talking to a woman who was dressed in biking clothes.

"Hey there, Lucas," Fiona called to me. "I want you to meet my friend Yolanda. She's been racing bicycles for the past ten years. I bet she can tell you a thing or two about getting fit. Heck, she could write a twenty-page paper on heart and lung endurance alone," said Fiona.

"I've learned about muscle endurance, but what's heart and lung endurance?" I asked.

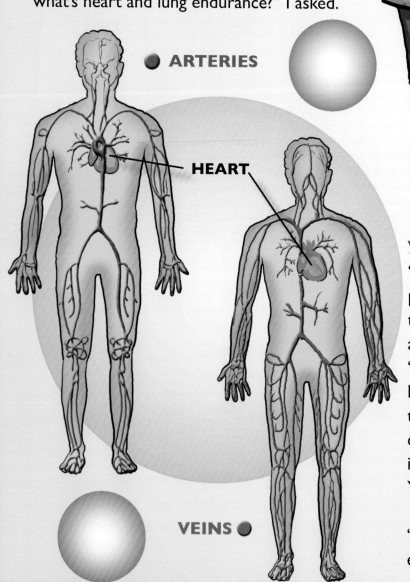

● **ARTERIES**

HEART

VEINS ●

YOU'VE GOT TO HAVE (A HEALTHY) HEART

"Well, young man, if you're going to be physically active, your heart and lungs have to be strong. Otherwise, they'll be strained, and you'll get tired quickly," said Yolanda. "You might not realize this, but your heart beats 100,000 times a day to pump blood through your arteries and veins. That blood carries oxygen from your lungs to every cell in your body to keep them working," Yolanda said.

"So how do I build my heart and lung endurance?" I asked.

A Slow Start to a Big Finish

Yolanda smiled. "All you really need to do is to perform activities that get your heart beating. The more you do these activities, the stronger your heart and lungs will become. Now, don't get me wrong, you don't have to go wild. In fact, it can be dangerous to get your heart rate up too high too quickly. You can walk at a quick pace to elevate your heart rate. Swimming is good, too. Me, I prefer biking to work out my heart and lungs."

Yolanda pointed outside to her bike which was leaning against the window. "The best thing that you can do is to get into a routine. I bike every day in the afternoon. It makes a big difference if you enjoy your exercise and start out slow. Over time, you'll be able to go faster and exercise for longer."

Slim Goodbody Says: Lucas can also build his lung and heart endurance by practicing the endurance run/walk part of the President's Challenge. This exercise measures the strength of your leg muscles and your heart and lung endurance.

Find a safe place, like a track or quiet street, where you can measure out a 1-mile (1.6km) distance. Time yourself as you run the mile. You can walk if you get tired. The more you practice, the faster you will get.

"I've always liked running. Maybe I can run after school a few days a week to work on my heart and lung endurance," I said.

"Sounds like a plan, kid. I'm headed out for a spin. Catch you later," said Yolanda.

THE FACTS OF FLEXIBILITY

The next week, I decided to go back to the gym. I had been lifting weights at home and running after school. Man, did my muscles hurt!

I found Fiona at the front desk. I winced as I walked up to her. "Hey, Fiona. Do you have any suggestions for taking care of sore muscles?"

"Have you been stretching before and after you work out?" Fiona asked, looking at me with concern.

"No, I've never been very good about stretching." I admitted.

STRETCH OUT TO STAY FIT

"Well, Lucas, flexibility and the ability to move your body easily and comfortably are an important part of being physically fit. Stretching helps protect your muscles and joints from injuries. You'll be amazed at how much more stable and flexible you'll feel if you stretch regularly. Swimming is another great way to stretch your muscles and joints. Yoga is great too. Have you ever taken a yoga class?" asked Fiona.

"No. Yoga doesn't seem like it will help me get strong and run faster though," I said.

"You're wrong about that, Lucas. Yoga strengthens your muscles as well as stretching them. If you do yoga, you'll have better balance, you'll be more flexible, and you won't get injured as easily. All of those things will make you a stronger athlete. Why don't you join the class at our fitness center? It sounds like you could use some flexibility training," Fiona said.

14

Slim Goodbody Says: Practicing yoga, martial arts, gymnastics, ballet, and *tai chi* are all great ways to strengthen and stretch your muscles and joints. Sign up for a class at your local Boys & Girls club or YMCA/YWCA and start your own flexibility training.

"Thanks Fiona. I guess I'll give the yoga class a try today." I said.

"That sounds good. And remember, just like the other parts of exercising, it's a good idea to start off slowly. If you stretch your muscles and joints too far too quickly, you can injure them."

Slim Goodbody Says: Lucas can also work on his flexibility by practicing the v-sit reach. This President's Challenge exercise measures the flexibility of your legs and back.

Mark a straight line 2 feet (61 cm) long on the floor as the baseline. Sit on the floor with your feet behind the line. Slowly reach forward as far as you can. Hold the stretch for 30 seconds.

15

BALANCE IS BEST

After a week of stretching before and after exercising, I was feeling much better. My muscles felt more relaxed and less sore. Before I went to bed that night, my mother reminded me that I had a doctor's appointment the next day.

The next afternoon, I told Dr. Robbins that I wanted to do better at the President's Challenge. I explained how I was trying to learn more about getting physically fit.

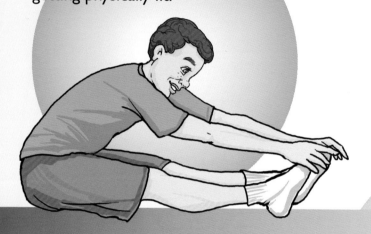

"Well that's great news, Lucas," responded Dr. Robbins. "Exercising regularly is an important part of developing a balanced **body composition**. You see, your body has both fat and lean **tissues**. Your body needs the fat to protect your organs from injury and to keep your body temperature stable. Your lean tissue includes your muscles, bones, nerves, skin, and organs. Your body composition is basically the amount of fat and lean tissue that you have. When you exercise, you help your body keep a healthy balance between its lean tissue and fat. If you're fit, you have more lean tissue and less fat."

Dr. Robbins pulled out the Move It chart.

Move It! *Choose your FUN!*

Do...

Your body counts on you to be active to help strengthen your bones and heart, and build muscles.

How much physical activity do kids need?

• GET AT LEAST 60 minutes a day of moderate activity, most days of the week.

LESS

Spend less time sitting around watching TV or using the computer.

ENOUGH

Do enough strengthening activities to keep your muscles firm.

MORE

Do more intense activities that warm you up and make you glow!

PLENTY

Walk, wiggle, dance, climb the stairs. Just keep moving whenever you can.

United States
Department of
Agriculture

Food and
Nutrition
Service

September 2000

See on the web: www.fns.usda.gov/tn/students

USDA is an equal opportunity provider and employer.

"Hey, my gym teacher showed me that chart," I said.

"It's a helpful guide. You can work toward a healthy body composition if you follow the chart and limit your time in front of the TV and computer. Instead, you need to spend time exercising and stretching and strengthening your muscles, heart, and lungs," explained Dr. Robbins.

Slim Goodbody Says: Try exercising while doing other activities. Stretch or pedal a stationary bike while watching television. When you are doing your homework, take breaks and do pushups and curl-ups. Try lifting weights when you talk on the phone. Get your family members to join in, too. You can even have competitions for the person who can do the most jumping jacks during a TV commercial. It's also a great idea to get your family outside. Exercising is often more fun with other people. Play tag, go hiking, or make a snowman. Playing outdoors is a great way to get exercise and to work toward a healthy body composition.

Treat Your Body Right

"Do you warm up for five or ten minutes before you exercise?" Dr. Robbins asked me.

"I've started stretching before I go for a run. It's helped a lot. My muscles don't feel as sore anymore, and my joints feel better, too," I told him.

"Stretching helps keep you from getting injured. Before you stretch, though, it's a good idea to warm up your muscles by slowly jogging in place for a few minutes. When you are finished exercising, you should also cool down gradually. You can jog slowly or walk for five to ten minutes to allow your heart and breathing to slow down. Then you can stretch your muscles. Of course, if you are riding a bike or going in-line skating, you can just ride or skate slowly to warm up and cool down before you stretch," explained Dr. Robbins.

WATER AND WHAT YOU WEAR

He continued, "While you exercise, your body loses a lot of fluid, because you are sweating. You must make sure that you drink water to replace those fluids."

"Is juice OK?" I asked.

"Actually, your body absorbs water much faster than it absorbs juice, so you should just drink water when you are exercising," said Dr. Robbins. "What kind of clothes and shoes do you wear when you exercise?"

"I just wear my jean shorts and some old running shoes," I said.

"You'll be much better off if you wear loose, comfortable clothing, Lucas. Cotton clothes work best, because they let air circulate. The moving air keeps your body temperature down. Shoes that fit well, support your ankles, and cushion your heels will also help prevent injuries. Ask your parents for a new pair of running shoes. They don't have to be fancy," suggested Dr. Robbins.

"OK," I said. "Thanks, Dr. Robbins."

"My pleasure, Lucas. And one more thing: Don't forget to take it easy when you are first getting in shape. Your body needs time to build strength. It's easy to give up on your fitness goals if you try to rush the first couple of weeks. Take it slowly and enjoy yourself," said Dr. Robbins.

COTTON

Slim Goodbody Says: A great way to know if you are exercising at a pace that is right for you is the talk-sing test. While you are exercising, try to talk to a friend. If you are too breathless to have a conversation, slow down. If you have enough energy to sing a song, try picking up the pace.

SMART, SAFE SPORTS

The next day, my friend Patrick came over to hang out. Patrick is a couple of years older than me, and I think of him as an older brother. He suggested that we go to the park to play in a roller-hockey game.

"Let me get my in-line skates and hockey stick," I said.

"Bring your wrist guards, knee pads, and a helmet, too. Without the right gear, it's really easy to get hurt. Some of the kids even wear elbow pads and mouth guards," said Patrick.

A CHALLENGE

When we arrived, we saw kids skating around and passing a ball with their hockey sticks. One of the kids on the rink shouted, "Hey, everyone, Lucas wants to play! This should be funny!"

"Don't listen to him," said Patrick, poking my arm with his elbow. "You're going to be great at this. They don't know that you've been getting in shape for the past three weeks. Let's show them what you're really made of!" Patrick carefully explained the rules of the game as we put on our equipment and warmed up.

Slim Goodbody Says: When players know the rules of the game — what's legal and what's not — fewer injuries happen. Everyone knows what to expect from each other. If you were playing touch football, you wouldn't tackle another player, right? Some rules focus more on being polite to the other players. It makes a big difference when players are respectful to one another and look out for each other.

THE BIG MOMENT

"OK, Lucas. This is it!" said Patrick. We skated onto the rink and took our positions. Suddenly, the ball zipped past me, and I wasn't nervous anymore. I raced after it and passed it to another teammate.

"Nice pass, Lucas," called Patrick. "Now get up there and score a goal!"

I skated as hard as I could. I was amazed to feel that my legs didn't burn with pain. They felt strong. I called for the ball, and one of my teammates passed it to me. I shot at the goal but missed the net.

"Darn it!" I shouted.

"Keep after it, Lucas!" hollered Patrick. The next time down the rink, I got the ball again. This time I knew I wouldn't miss. I hit the ball as hard as I could, and my teammates started cheering!

They shouted, "Nice goal, Lucas! Where did you learn a slap shot like that? You can play with us anytime!"

HEALTHY CHOICES

Partway through the game, two of the players ran into each other. One of them twisted his knee. He sat on the ground, holding his leg and wincing in pain.

"Jimmy, you should sit out the rest of the game," said Patrick to the injured boy.

"No way, I'm fine. Just give me a second," groaned Jimmy.

"Jimmy, you can't exercise when you get hurt. You've got to give your injury a chance to heal," said Patrick.

"Come on, Patrick, I just want to play," said Jimmy.

Slim Goodbody Says: Patrick is right. You should not exercise if you're injured. If you don't rest an injury, it will take your body much longer to heal. Use the R.I.C.E. treatment to take care of an injury and to reduce pain and swelling.

Rest whatever body part is hurt.

Ice — Put a cold pack, ice cubes, or frozen vegetables where it hurts.

Compression — Wrap the injured body part with a bandage.

Elevate the injured area. Place it on a pillow so that it is above your heart.

A Plan for Decisions

"Patrick is right," said one of the other older players who was named Tom. "You've got to make smart decisions about injuries. My dad taught me a little tool that helps me make good decisions. I use it to make sure that I am making the best decision for my future, rather than basing my decision on what I want at that moment. First, you *identify your choices*. Next, you *evaluate each choice* and think about their consequences. Then, you *identify the healthiest decision and take action*, and finally, you evaluate your decision," said Tom.

"So my choices are to play or sit out," said Jimmy.

"Right. Now, evaluate those choices. If you play, your knee might take longer to heal. If you sit out, you'll only miss part of the game. So which do you think is the healthiest decision?" asked Tom.

"I guess I'd better sit out," said Jimmy. He hobbled off the rink to elevate his leg. After the game was over, we gathered around Jimmy. His knee was swelling up, but he seemed okay.

A Good Decision

"It was a good idea to take a rest," Jimmy said, evaluating his choice. "I didn't realize how badly I had twisted it. I should get home and ice and elevate it more before it becomes even more swollen. See you guys later."

Slim Goodbody Says: Learning how to make healthy decisions is an important skill. The next time you are exercising, use these five steps to make healthy decisions.
- Identify your choices
- Evaluate each choice, thinking about the consequences of each choice
- Identify the healthiest decision
- Take action
- Evaluate your decision

GOOD GOALS

After the game, we stretched our muscles and started walking home. I felt great. "That was really fun," I told Patrick. "Thanks for inviting me."

"You played really well. I think your running and weightlifting are really paying off," said Patrick.

"I hope so, but I'm worried that I won't be ready for the President's Challenge at school. It's only a few weeks away, and I still feel like I have a long way to go," I worried.

STEPS TO SUCCESS

"Do you have a specific goal for the President's Challenge?" asked Patrick.

"A specific goal?" I asked.

"Yeah. My mom is a track coach, and she always tells me that it helps to set goals when I am trying to accomplish something. It's really easy. First, you *set a realistic and specific goal and write it down*. Then, you *list the steps to*

reach the goal. Then, you *get help and support from others*. Then, you *evaluate your progress*, and finally, you *reward yourself*.

"Geez, I never thought about setting a goal. I just want to do well," I said.

"It helps a lot if your goals are measurable. What if you set a goal to reach a certain **percentile**?" suggested Patrick.

TO BE IN THE TOP HALF

"That sounds good. Okay, my goal is to be in the 50th percentile or above in all of the events." I said. "I'm also going to work on beating my own record from last year. I want to do twice as many repetitions of every exercise and take a minute off of my running time for the mile!"

"It'll be easy to evaluate your progress when we get tested in the President's Challenge," replied Patrick. "Ms. Lindsay will tell you what percentile you reach, your running time, and the number of repetitions that you did. But before we get to the Challenge, what do you think you need to do to reach those goals?"

"Well, I guess if I run or go skating three times a week and and keep doing my pushups,

bicep curl-ups, and heel raises, I'll be ready." I answered.

"Do you need any help from me or your family?" Patrick asked.

"Well, it would be a lot easier to stick with my plan and more fun if someone would exercise with me." I said.

"I'll go in-line skating with you. How about every Tuesday and Thursday evening?" offered Patrick. "We've got one more big question — how will you reward yourself if you reach your goal?"

"I think I'll buy myself some weights so I don't have to use soup cans anymore," I grinned.

Slim Goodbody Says: Now it's time for you to set a specific fitness goal! Remember, make your goal realistic and measurable, and follow Patrick's goal-setting steps:
• Set a realistic goal and write it down
• List the steps to reach the goal
• Get help and support from others
• Evaluate your progress
• Reward yourself

AN ADVOCATE FOR HEALTH

The weeks went by quickly. Before I knew it, I was in gym class, warming up for the President's Challenge. I felt strong and flexible, and I had been eating healthy foods for weeks. During each event, I could feel my muscles working. I was sweating and breathing hard, but I was doing better than I expected. My friends watched me in amazement.

"What's gotten into you, Lucas?" asked one of them.

"I've been getting ready for this for the past ten weeks," I told them happily.

At the end of the day, Ms. Lindsay found me. "Lucas, I'm so impressed. You really are a lean, mean, fitness machine!" she laughed. "You were in the 85th percentile or above in every event. I'm happy to present you with the Presidential Physical Fitness Award! Congratulations!"

"Yes!" I shouted, pumping my arms. "I did it!"

HELPING OUT OTHERS

"Lucas, would you ever consider becoming a health advocate?" Ms. Lindsay asked.

"What's that?" I responded.

"A health advocate is someone who works to make his or her family, school, and community healthier and stronger. First, you *take a healthy stand on an issue*. Then you work to *persuade others to make a healthy choice*. And most importantly, you have to *be convincing*," Ms. Lindsay explained.

"Well, I sure believe in the importance of being physically fit. After the last ten weeks, I know it's challenging, but it feels great. I would love to help some of my friends get in shape, too. Many of them would rather play video games than go for a run," I said.

"How do you think you could persuade them to make healthier choices?" she asked.

"Well, I guess I could invite them to exercise with me. I can show them how fun getting in shape can be," I said.

"Do you think you can be convincing?" Ms. Lindsay asked.

"I know I can! I can tell them how important it is to exercise and to keep their hearts and lungs healthy. I can also let them know about the health problems that they could face if they don't exercise regularly," I said.

"You're going to be a great health advocate, Lucas. Good luck!" said Ms. Lindsay.

Slim Goodbody Says: You can become a health advocate too! Invite your friends to walk to school with you or start up activity clubs, such as hiking clubs or basketball or baseball teams and leagues.

BODIES BUILT FOR MOVEMENT

After school, Patrick and I walked to the athletic store to buy a set of 5- and 10-pound hand weights. I was so excited to reward myself for achieving my goal in the President's Challenge.

"Ms. Lindsay asked me to become a health advocate and teach my friends about the value of exercise," I told Patrick.

"Are you going to do it?" he asked.

"The truth is, I wish everyone would get in shape. I can't believe how much better I feel. My muscles, lungs, and heart all feel great when I exercise. I'm a lot more flexible than I used to be, too. I feel more confident, as well. I guess people need to exercise their bodies to feel the best they can!"

"Yeah, but all of our friends sit around and play video games all day," laughed Patrick.

SET A GOAL, BUT START SLOW

"I know! I learned from my doctor that when you don't exercise, you can have an unhealthy body composition. That means that your body has more fat than it has lean tissue. He told me that people who don't exercise can have serious health problems. I mean, I know how hard it can be to start getting in shape. Your legs burn, and it is difficult to catch your breath when you go for a run. But now I know that if you set goals, start slowly, and have an exercise routine that you follow each week, it's a lot easier to get through the first couple of weeks," I said.

"It's easy for me because I love skating. I guess every person needs to find some kind of exercise that he or she enjoys," offered Patrick.

"I think Tom's advice about making healthy decisions is good, too. His decision-making tool could help people get off the couch."

"Yeah, and as long as people wear the right gear and take care of themselves when they are injured, they'll be able to have fun getting in shape." I said. "You know, Patrick, I think I'm going to become a health advocate. I'll be like the superhero of health, Lucas the lean, mean, fitness machine!"

GOOD HEALTH

Don't forget to drink a lot of water while exercising. Be sure to warm up, cool down, and stretch your muscles, too!

LUCAS

Slim Goodbody Says: What have you discovered about physical fitness and good health by reading this book? Take some time to consider what you have learned and then make a poster encouraging people to get active and about the importance of getting fit. You can put your poster up at school to remind everyone why it is important to exercise.

Glossary

abdominal Describes the region of the body between the chest and the hips, also known as the belly

aerobic Means "with oxygen", and refers to how a muscle produces energy by using oxygen. Aerobic exercises are performed at a low to moderate level of intensity over a long time

body composition How much lean and fat tissue is in one's body

calories Units of food energy; calories that are not burned through physical activity or everyday life are stored in the body as fat

cell A tiny unit that is the basic building block of all living things

diabetes A condition in which people have too much sugar in their blood. People with diabetes cannot produce enough insulin, the substance that the body needs to use sugar properly

endurance The ability to withstand physical activity for long periods of time

flexibility The ability to bend easily without injury

high blood pressure A condition that forces the heart to work harder to pump blood

FOR MORE INFORMATION

BAM Body and Mind Website by the Center for Disease Control

www.bam.gov/sub_physicalactivity/index.html

Get expert advice, learn the rules of many sports, see how athletes overcome physical challenges and more on this government website.

Kidnetic

www.kidnetic.com

Check out this website for fitness challenges, to try out a fitness scavenger hunt, and to learn other fun ways to exercise and stay fit.

The President's Challenge

www.presidentschallenge.org/home_kids.aspx

Learn more about the physical activities of the President's Challenge and win awards for finishing an exercise program.

United States Food and Drug Administration: Eat Smart Play Hard- Kids

www.fns.usda.gov/eatsmartplayhardkids

Play games and learn new exercises on this animated, fun website.

ABOUT THE AUTHOR

John Burstein (also known as Slim Goodbody) has been entertaining and educating children for over thirty years. His programs have been broadcast on CBS, PBS, Nickelodeon, USA, and Discovery. He has won numerous awards including the Parent's Choice Award and the President's Council's Fitness Leader Award. Currently, Mr. Burstein tours the country with his live multimedia show "Bodyology." For more information, please visit slimgoodbody.com